LISTEN TO THE SPIRIT

AS HE SPEAKS TO YOUTH

by
Dick Hillis

*General Director of
Overseas Crusades, Inc.*

and

Don W. Hillis

*Associate Director of
The Evangelical Alliance Mission
(TEAM)*

BAKER BOOK HOUSE
Grand Rapids, Michigan

ISBN: 0-8010-4080-9

Contents

THIS BOOK
IS WRITTEN IN THE FIRST PERSON
AS IF THE HOLY SPIRIT
WERE THE AUTHOR.
WE BELIEVE
THIS WILL ENABLE YOU
TO SEE MORE CLEARLY
HOW PERSONALLY INTERESTED
THE HOLY SPIRIT IS
IN YOU.

The seven-pointed star is often used as a symbol for the Holy Spirit. Each point stands for one of His gifts as mentioned in the Book of Revelation: power, wisdom, riches, strength, honor, glory, and blessing.

You and I

MY NAME is Holy Spirit . . . "Spirit" because I am a living personality . . . "Holy" because I am the Spirit of God. I have other names, too. Sometimes I am called the Comforter and sometimes the Spirit of truth. These names reveal something of my character and my activities. (Don't let the word *Spirit* throw you. You too are a spirit, only you are living in a house of flesh and bones.)

You have heard preachers speak of the Father, the Son, and the Holy Spirit. Because I am last on the list, you may have come to think of me as a little less God than the Father and the Son, but we are all equally God. We simply have different work to do. So when you think of Father, Son, and Holy Spirit, think of us as equals.

I don't usually talk about myself. I would rather talk about Jesus. But it is important that you come to know me like I know you, for I am the one who makes it possible for you to live the life you want to live in Christ.

Let's start at the beginning, or before the beginning, because being God I have neither beginning nor end. I want you to know that thousands of years ago I had a part in the creation of the universe. "The earth was at first a shapeless, chaotic mass, with the Spirit of God brooding over the dark vapors" (Gen. 1:2, *TLB*). Furthermore, all through the Old Testament I was the one who directed the lives of the prophets of God. I enabled them to perform miracles and declare prophecies. I, through Moses, brought the plagues upon Egypt. I taught the secrets of God to Daniel and gave him wisdom to interpret forgotten dreams.

Nebuchadnezzar was the mightiest ruler of the Babylonian Empire. In his second year as emperor, he had a dream that really bugged him. He called his magicians, sorcerers, and astrologers together and ordered them to tell him what his dream was about and then interpret for him the meaning of the dream. In their helplessness they replied, "There is not a man upon the earth that can shew the king's matter . . ." (Dan. 2:10). Their answer so angered Nebuchadnezzar that he "commanded to destroy all the wise men of Babylon" (Dan. 2:12).

All too soon Arioch, the military captain, came to take Daniel, as he was considered one of the wise men of the kingdom. Daniel bravely went to the enraged monarch and told him that he would tell him the dream and give the interpretation if the king would simply grant him a little time. The king agreed and Daniel returned to his house and with his three friends prayed that God would reveal the secret. That very night the secret was revealed to Daniel.

It was natural, even before going to the king, that Daniel should praise God: "Blessed be the name of God for ever and ever: for wisdom and might are his" (Dan. 2:20). "He reveals profound mysteries beyond man's understanding. He knows all hidden things, for he is light, and darkness is no obstacle to him" (Dan. 2:22, *TLB*).

The following day Arioch brought Daniel in before the monarch. The king asked Daniel if he was able to make known the dream and then to interpret it. Daniel replied, "No wise man, astrologer, magician, or wizard can tell the king such things; but there is a God in heaven who reveals secrets, and he has told you in your dream what will happen in the future" (Dan. 2:27, 28, *TLB*).

Daniel then told the king his dream and interpreted its meaning. When Daniel finished, the king was so shook that he fell on his face and said, "Truly, O Daniel, . . . your God is the God of gods, Ruler of kings, the Revealer of mysteries, because he has told you this secret" (Dan. 2:47, *TLB*).

In the New Testament I led Jesus into the wilderness for the forty days of temptation He faced in Satan's presence. It was in reliance upon me that Jesus walked and performed all His miracles on earth. It was also through my mighty power that He was raised from the dead. Jesus' life of dependence upon me was to demonstrate that when a child of God lives in complete reliance on and obedience to me he can live the victorious life God wants him to live. It was also through me and in the name of Jesus that the apostles carried on their ministry of miracles.

Take by way of illustration the healing of the lame man at the beautiful gate of the temple. Peter and John were going to a prayer meeting at the temple. At the gate a poor man, lame from birth, begged for a coin. Peter's reply was, "Silver and gold have I none; but such as I have give I thee: In the name of Jesus Christ of Nazareth rise up and walk" (Acts 3:6). The result was immediate and spectacular, for the lame man leaped up and walked and, of course, praised God. All the people around the temple saw him walking and praising God. This angered some of the religious leaders so much that they put Peter and John in jail overnight. The following morning they brought the two disciples before the high court to ask them how they had performed such a miracle. "Then Peter, *filled with the Holy Ghost, said,* . . . by the name of Jesus Christ of Nazareth . . . even by him doth this man stand here before you whole" (Acts 4:8-10).

You see, when Jesus left His disciples and went back to the Father, I took His place here on earth. Jesus came from heaven to earth to make salvation for all men possible. I came to bring men to Christ and then to make the victorious life in Christ a reality to those who accept the Savior.

Even before His crucifixion Jesus promised the disciples that He would send me. When He told them that He would be leaving soon, they really got upset. But Jesus assured them He would not leave them "orphans." His words to them were, "And I will pray the Father, and he shall give you another Comforter" (John 14:16). While Jesus was with them, He was their provision, protection, and

13

comfort. He reassured them through His promise of "another Comforter." (The Greek word for *another* means "one like unto myself.") Jesus was saying to them that everything He had done while with them I would do when the Father sent me to indwell them. He even declared that "It is best for you that I go away, for if I don't, the Comforter won't come . . ." (John 16:7, *TLB*). You see how much importance Jesus placed on my coming to earth).

Jesus was with His disciples only three short years. He promised, however, that I would remain with believers as long as they existed, "that he [the Holy Spirit] may abide with you *for ever.*" What could be more wonderful and reassuring than God being with a person forever? So it is that in Jesus' last talk with His disciples before the crucifixion He said, "I will send him unto you." Then following His resurrection from the grave and just before His ascension, Jesus made the point again: "But ye shall receive power, after that the Holy Ghost is come upon you: and ye shall be witnesses unto me both in Jerusalem, and in all Judaea, and in Samaria, and unto the uttermost part of the earth" (Acts 1:8).

Jesus' true disciples believed their Savior's promise. Ten days later I came to indwell them. From that moment it was no longer

14

God with them, or God in front of them, or God beside them, or God above them, but God *in* them. Now you understand why Jesus said it would be better. If you have accepted Jesus Christ as your Savior, then I, the Holy Spirit, indwell you and your body is my temple and I make it possible for you to live the Christian life. The fact is, without me it would be impossible for you to be a Christian, but more about that in the next chapter.

Your Birth and I

You would not be a Christian today if it were not for my work. Jesus said I would come into the world to "reprove the world of sin, and of righteousness, and of judgment" (John 16:8). The word *reprove* means "to convince or probe." When a doctor is caring for a bad case of leprosy, it is often necessary for him to cut away rotting flesh. Because leprosy deadens the nerves, he has to probe until he touches a live nerve. The patient is then quick to let the doctor know when he touches a sore spot.

16

You may or may not have lived a life of deep sin. In any case, you have lived a life separated from God, for everyone has broken the laws of God, and the breaking of His laws separates man from Him. You may feel you are a good person. You may be a church member. You may have participated in the sacraments of the church and yet, without my probing, convicting work, you cannot be saved.

Think, for example, of a man and a woman whose stories are recorded in the New Testament. Let's take the man first. His friends called him Nick but his parents called him Nicodemus. His name means "above, superior to the people." His parents were ambitious that he should become an outstanding leader in his nation. He did not disappoint them. He lived to become one of the seventy top men of his nation. He was a ruler of the Jews (John 3:1) and also a Pharisee (a man of deep religious convictions). But with all his success and warm religious habits, I made him so uncomfortable that he knew something was missing. As I continued to probe, he became so uneasy that he decided to risk his reputation and go and talk to Jesus.

Jesus was lovingly blunt and got right to the point of telling him, "Ye must be born again" (John 3:7)—another way of saying, "You must be converted." Nicodemus understood his human birth but was puzzled by any second birth type of experience. So Jesus explained, "That which is born of the flesh is flesh [natural birth]; and that which is born of the Spirit is spirit [a supernatural birth]" (John 3:6). Nicodemus wanted to know how this could be and Jesus patiently explained, "Except a man be born of water and of the Spirit, he cannot enter into the kingdom of God" (John 3:5). Jesus was informing Nicodemus that the new birth is the miracle of my work. I use the Word of God to probe and convict until men acknowledge their sin and their need of a Savior. Nicodemus acknowledged that all his religious practices had not saved him. He admitted an inner emptiness had to be filled and he believed on Jesus as his Savior.

In the story immediately following that of the conversion of the religious man, Nicodemus, there is a story of a very irreligious Samaritan woman. Her life was a sad mess, filled with sin, frustrations, and deep disappointments. She sought happiness and peace of heart through five marriages and found nothing but grief and dissatisfaction. Jesus met her at the well of Sychar and began to talk with her. As He talked I probed. Soon she confessed her life of lust and sin and wanted to know how she could be set free from the chains of bondage she had forged.

So deep became her conviction that Jesus was the Savior (Messiah) she so desperately needed that, leaving her waterpot, she hurried to the city to tell her people she had found forgiveness of sin through faith in Jesus Christ. So convincing was her testimony that "many of the Samaritans of that city believed on him for the saying of the woman . . ." (John 4:39). Their faith was a result of my work in their hearts.

Those conversions took place in Asia. Now let me tell you of the first conversions in Europe. They are important to you, for the way of salvation reached you through the converts in Europe.

The human instruments I used were two missionaries, Paul and Silas. Philippi, a chief city in Greece, was their first stop. They learned that a little group of people was meeting every Saturday for prayer. The prayer meeting wasn't held in a building. It was a small group of women meeting in a quiet place down by the riverside. The two missionaries joined the women and told them of the life, the miracles, the death, and the resurrection of Christ.

As they spoke I prodded the tender heart of a business woman named Lydia. She immediately responded to my convicting work and there on the river bank she became a new creature in Christ Jesus (II Cor. 5:17). Now she wanted to do something for the Lord's servants so she invited them to leave their hotel and live with her family during their stay in Philippi. Paul and Silas gladly accepted her invitation and every day went from her home out on the streets preaching.

The second convert was a young girl possessed with "a spirit of Python." She was demon possessed and made her owners a lot of money through soothsaying (fortunetelling). The spirit who possessed her recognized Paul and Silas as Christian missionaries and kept crying out, "These men are the servants of the most high God, which shew unto us the way of salvation" (Acts 16:17). Finally Paul turned to the girl and said to the evil spirit, "I command thee in the name of Jesus Christ to come out of her. And he came out the same hour" (Acts 16:18).

She responded to my convicting work and became the second convert in Europe. But don't think that the men who owned the girl were pleased. They were so angry they turned the missionaries over to the police. In prison Paul and Silas were stripped to the waist, beaten with many stripes, and their feet locked in the stocks. Such treatment should have silenced any preacher, but Paul and Silas spent the night praying and singing praises unto God. They not only kept their fellow prisoners awake but God heard them and sent a local earthquake, which so shook the foundations of the prison that the doors flew open.

The shaking of the earth also snapped the bands that held the prisoners. This so frightened the jailer that he took his sword and was going to kill himself. Paul shouted to him that none of the prisoners had fled and therefore there was no reason for him to commit suicide. He ran to Paul and Silas, fell on his knees, and asked, "Sirs, what must I do to be saved?" (Acts 16:30). The jailer's heart was prepared by me and I led Paul to give a simple answer, "Believe on the Lord Jesus Christ, and thou shalt be saved" (Acts 16:31). Through my convicting work this jailer was the third convert in Europe and then came his whole family. So the Word of God spread and the number of believers increased.

You see, I can work with the very religious and the very irreligious and all those in between. And if any will respond to my probing and convicting and repent, they will be converted. In my probing I use many means. I may use a hymn, a poem, a verse of Scripture, a testimony, or a kind act. You can trust me. I will use every method possible to get every person possible to accept Jesus.

Your Body and I

Part 1

At the moment of your conversion, I made my home in you and your body became my temple. In writing to the young believers in Corinth, Paul said concerning me, "Haven't you yet learned that your body is the home of the Holy Spirit God gave you, and that He lives within you?" (I Cor. 6:19, *TLB*). It must be wonderful for you to realize that your body with its weakness, disease, and tremendous capacity for good or evil has become my temple . . . a dwelling place for the living God.

The following verses suggest divine ownership: "Your own body does not belong to you. For God has bought you with a great price. So use every part of your body to give glory back to God, because He owns it" (I Cor. 6:19, 20, *TLB*).

Your life is now under "new management," for you have been redeemed at a very high price: "Forasmuch as ye know that ye were not redeemed with corruptible things, as silver and gold . . . But with the precious blood of Christ . . ." (I Pet. 1:18, 19). The word *redeemed* means "bought." Man once belonged to God. But through obedience to Satan and disobedience to God, he became a slave of Satan. The price needed to deliver man from his slave master was death. Someone qualified must meet and satisfy God's holy demands. Christ did exactly that.

Because Christ is man He could die for man. Because He is God His death counted for all mankind. Get this—Christ did not pay the price to Satan, for Satan is a usurper. Christ paid the price to God. Every time you look at Christ dying on the cross, you should see what He paid to God to buy you back from the slavery of sin. Is it then any wonder that Scripture says, "Therefore glorify God in your body, and in your spirit, which are God's"? (I Cor. 6:20)

How does one glorify God in his body? First, he must allow no idols. Anything in one's life that takes first place (the place God should have) becomes a personal idol. "And what agreement hath the temple of God with idols?" (II Cor. 6:16).

Scripture records the story of a well-to-do Christian who lived on the island of Cyprus. His name was Barnabas. Money might very easily have become his idol. But Barnabas sold his land and gave his money to the missionaries for their work.

A Christian couple who saw what praise this brought to Barnabas also sold their land. They received such a hefty price for it they decided to give only part of the money to the missionaries but to pretend it was the total amount they had received. The missionary, Peter, saw through it and said, "Why hath Satan filled thine heart to lie to the Holy Ghost?" (Acts 5:3). You see, "love of money" was their idol and with their idolatry came deceit and lying. The apostle John warns Christians, "Little children, keep yourselves from idols" (I John 5:21).

Second, to glorify God in your body and in your spirit, you must keep your body and spirit cleansed from sin. As your holy Lord I cannot stand unholy things in my temple. Paul puts it this way, "And grieve not the holy Spirit of God..." (Eph. 4:30). How would you grieve an immaculate housekeeper? One way is to walk through her clean house with muddy boots. You grieve me by bringing sin into your body, which is my temple. If in your heart I find covetousness, jealousy, lust, unbelief, materialism, hypocrisy, and other such things, I am grieved.

Take unbelief. Do you remember the record of Peter's fall? Let me refresh your memory. Jesus had been betrayed by Judas and was arrested and taken to the high priest's house for trial. Peter followed at a safe distance and finally sat down in the courtyard with the enemies of Jesus. A young lady recognized Peter and accused him of being one of Jesus' disciples. Peter's lying answer was, "Woman, I know him not" (Luke 22:57). Three times Peter was questioned about his relationship to Christ and three times he denied that he knew Him. Jesus was wounded and I was grieved. But Peter was not the only follower of Jesus who grieved me.

Following Jesus' resurrection He appeared to His disciples. Thomas was away at the time. When he returned the disciples all told him the thrilling news that Christ had risen from the grave and had visited them. In raw unbelief, Thomas said, "Except I shall see in his hands the print of the nails, and put my finger into the print of the nails, and thrust my hand into his side, I will not believe"

(John 20:25). The unbelief of Thomas was as bad as Peter's denial, and it grieved me. Have you ever denied Jesus as Peter did? Have you, like Thomas, ever said, "I will not believe"?

Third, if you are to glorify God in your body and spirit, which are the Lord's, I must not be quenched (I Thess. 5:19). The word *quench* means "to put out." As the landlord of your life, it is my business to direct you in such a way as to bring glory to God. I am in charge of your daily life. I alone make it possible for you to live the life in Christ.

Therefore, the word is "Walk in [by means of] the Spirit, and ye shall not fulfil the lust of the flesh" (Gal. 5:16). To walk in the Spirit is real liberty. You get up in the morning and turn your spirit and body over to me and ask me to direct your every move and to guide all your conversations. As long as you obey my inward promptings, you are "walking in the Spirit." Your spiritual life is nurtured and maintained only through me. I alone enable you to live the overflowing life.

Again we turn to Scripture for an illustration. On the last day of the Feast of Tabernacles, the people followed the priest down to the Pool of Siloam. There they filled their jugs with water. Then they returned to the temple and sang, "Behold, God is my salvation; I will trust, and not be afraid: for the Lord JEHOVAH is my strength and my song;

26

he also is become my salvation. Therefore with joy shall ye draw water out of the wells of salvation" (Isa. 12:2, 3).

Then they poured their water on the hot pavement. This was a symbolic act. It indicated that the worshiper was pouring his life out in commitment to God. One day as they were going through their ceremony, Jesus spoke up and said, "If any man thirst, let him come unto me, and drink. He that believeth on me . . . out of his belly shall flow rivers of living water. (But this spake he of the Spirit)" (John 7:37-39).

Your body is to be a holy temple, from which my overflowing life flows. Too many are water jug Christians. They work so hard and dry up so quickly. In a crisis they panic and go to pieces. I have a new kind of life for you. Just as a river is effortless as it flows, just as a river grows deeper the farther it flows, just as a river brings life to everything it touches, so it will be with you when you commit your daily life to my Lordship and direction.

Philip, the deacon, illustrates this obedient Spirit-filled life I have for you. Scripture says that he was a man of "honest report, full of the Holy Ghost and wisdom" (Acts 6:3). First he faithfully served the church in Jerusalem. Then I called him to go work among the despised Samaritans, and he obeyed me. The result of his Spirit-filled obedient life was that "the people with one accord gave heed unto those things which Philip spake" (Acts 8:6).

I used Philip in such a way as to gather a great harvest among the Samaritans. In the midst of the harvest, Philip was given an assignment to leave and go to Gaza, which is desert. No questions asked, he went. While on the road he saw the treasurer of Ethiopia returning home from Jerusalem in his chariot. I said unto Philip, "Go near, and join thyself to this chariot" (Acts 8:29). Again Philip gave unquestioning obedience to my bidding and as a result he led the great man to Christ. Philip glorified God in his body and his life was blessed and fruitful. I have the same kind of life for you if you will live as Philip did.

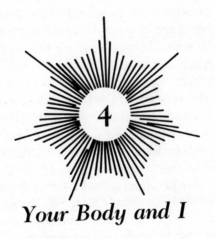

Your Body and I

Part 2

"You would not be a Christian today if it were not for my work." Sound familiar? These were the opening words of Chapter 2. They try to say exactly what the last half of Romans 8:9 tells you: "And remember that if anyone doesn't have the Spirit of Christ living in him, he is not a Christian at all" (*TLB*). One of the great distinctives of Christianity is that I, the Spirit of God, live in human bodies. You won't find such wonderful teaching in Islam, Hinduism, Buddhism, or any of the other great religions.

But perhaps you have some questions as to whether I really live in your body. In that case, let me give you a check list which will help you find the answer. I'm sure you will discover there is more evidence of my presence in your life than you may have previously guessed.

The fact of my presence in you is based upon the promise of Christ. You have already been reminded that Jesus told His disciples the Father would send me to be with you, in you, and to lead you into all truth. So the reality of my presence is built on Christ's word. Furthermore, you know that promise was fulfilled fifty days after Christ returned to heaven on a day called Pentecost. My coming into the believers at Jerusalem was just as real as the birth of Jesus in Bethlehem. He first appeared in a stable and I first came to earth in an upper room in Jerusalem. It is pretty difficult to account for the history of the church apart from my presence in the lives of God's people.

But all that may sound a little distant. There is a very deep and subjective evidence that your body is my temple. It is expressed in these words: "For his Holy Spirit speaks to us deep in our hearts, and tells us that we really are God's children" (Rom. 8:16, *TLB*).

Part of my work in your life is to give you the assurance of my presence. I do it by whispering to your heart that you are mine and that I live within you. You may recognize this as a "deep inner confidence," a "feeling of peace and joy," or a "steadfast trust." Regardless of how you express it, you know you have an inner strength and faith which are given you by someone other than yourself. You are sensitive to the fact that there are times when I speak to you and you to me.

This leads to a third very meaningful evidence of the fact that your body is my temple. It relates to the subject of guidance. Romans 8:14 reads, "For all who are led by the Spirit of God are sons of God" (*TLB*). Even a hasty study of the Book of Acts reveals ways in which I guided Christ's servants to be at the right place at the right time to do the right jobs.

Paul, Peter, Philip, Stephen, and many others proved they were children of God as they responded to my directives. There were times they wanted to move in other directions (Acts 16), but I kept them on the right paths.

You will find it a healthy exercise to ask yourself, "Am I walking in the Spirit?" By repeatedly checking on yourself, you will become sensitive to my guidance. You will be amazed at how often, even in apparently insignificant matters, you will find yourself at

31

the right place doing the right thing or saying the right words. "Walking in the Spirit" can be an exciting experience for you. I am, after all, in a good position to give you the kind of guidance that will make your life meaningful and will glorify Jesus Christ. If you will check on the lives of men God has used, you will find this is true.

Christian victory is another thing that signals my presence in the life of a person. You are reminded in Romans 8 that you have no obligation to live according to the dictates of your old, sinful nature. On the contrary, you are to crush your old nature and its evil deeds "through the power of the Holy Spirit" (Rom. 8:13, *TLB*). I don't have to tell you that the world, the flesh, and the devil are strong and vicious enemies. You have already discovered that. You have also learned that you are not able to overcome any one of them by yourself.

Like Paul, you have probably often said, "It seems to be a fact of life that when I want to do what is right, I inevitably do what is wrong. I love to do God's will so far as my new nature is concerned; But there is something else deep within me, in my lower nature, that is at war with my mind and wins the fight and makes me a slave to the sin that is still within me. In my mind I want to be

God's willing servant but instead I find myself still enslaved to sin" (Rom. 7:21-25, *TLB*).

The answer to your struggles lies in the fact that I live within you both to will and to do God's good pleasure. This includes the task of making you a victorious Christian. You can only be triumphant with my help. This doesn't mean you will live a sinless life. I will say more about that in another chapter.

Fruitfulness is another word that points to my presence in your life. This relates to your character. It refers to the fact that I produce certain characteristics within you which are beyond and something more than those which are normal to you. Galatians 5:22, 23 expresses it in this way: "But when the Holy Spirit controls our lives He will produce this kind of fruit in us: love, joy, peace, patience, kindness, goodness, faithfulness, gentleness and self-control" (*TLB*).

When I am in control of your life, there will be a certain Christlikeness in evidence. Anyone who says he is a Christian ought to live like the Lord Jesus Christ. This means you are to be like Him in His love for people, in His humility, in His gentleness, in His honesty, and in many other ways. But, of course, this is impossible apart from my presence in you.

Your spiritual appetites are another evidence that your body is my temple. Your

33

desire for prayer has not come from natural sources. Your "old nature" does not seek after spiritual benefits. I am the Spirit of prayer and you do your best praying when you "pray in the Spirit." Romans 8:26 says, "The Holy Spirit helps us with our daily problems and in our praying. For we don't even know what we should pray for, nor how to pray as we should; but the Holy Spirit prays for us with such feeling that it cannot be expressed in words" (TLB).

How do you explain your hunger for and understanding of God's Word? It is not a characteristic of an unregenerate nature. Nor does it primarily depend on your mental acumen. It depends on your relationship with me. An appetite for prayer, Bible study, and Christian fellowship is irrefutable proof that your body is my temple. You are a healthy, growing Christian because you are responding to that appetite.

The last evidence that your body is my temple is seen in the spiritual contribution you make to your fellow Christians. I give to each child of God a gift or a tool for him to use in serving Christ. The names of some of those tools have been listed in I Corinthians 12 and 14. Others are recorded in Romans 12 and in Ephesians 5. These lists include most of the tools I give to believers for the purpose of building and strengthening all those who make up the body of Christ. Because I know the best way in which you can be of service to Christ, I select the tool and give it to you. It is then your privilege to use that gift for the building up of fellow Christians and for the ongoing of the gospel.

Check the lists carefully. If you are not sure what my gift is for you, then ask me and I will be glad to show you what it is. You will be your happiest when you know you are using my gift to you for God's glory. And right here let me assure you that I love you with infinite love. I can neither do more nor less than that.

So there you have it . . . some clearcut evidences of my presence in your life. How do they all add up with you?

Your Bible and I

Part 1

I am your divine landlord. You are my temple. I am God. You are man. As Christ came to earth and took upon Himself a human body, so I came to earth to indwell human bodies. Christ indwelt a physical body that He might be able to die for lost mankind. I indwell human bodies to make the life of Christ a possibility. How do I help you?

First, I am your teacher or professor. Without me you could not so much as understand the life in Christ. The Bible declares, "But the natural man receiveth not the things of the Spirit of God: for they are foolishness unto him: neither can he know them, because they are spiritually discerned" (I Cor. 2:14). But Jesus made His disciples the following promise about me, "Howbeit when he, the Spirit of truth, is come, he will guide you into all truth . . ." (John 16:13). I am the *Spirit of God* . . . the *Spirit of grace* . . . the *Spirit of truth*.

Truth is the freeing agent of life. "Ye shall know the truth and the truth shall make you free." I set you free from mental and spiritual bondage. I am the one who "guides you into all truth." I guard you from the errors of cults and isms. My teaching goes deeper than head knowledge. I teach you spiritual truth and then cause you to enter into it experientially. I do not mean to imply that you don't need to listen to good preachers or that you don't need to attend good Bible studies. Indeed, I am the one who teaches the human preacher or teacher. He is the vessel I use.

"For what man knoweth the things of a man, save the spirit of man which is in him? even so the things of God knoweth no man, but the *Spirit of God*" (II Cor. 2:11). When it comes to the "things of God," I alone am your real teacher. I alone can interpret God to you. A seminary president once said to his student body, "I would rather you had five minutes of the Holy Spirit's teaching than a sheepskin from this seminary." He was not downgrading the seminary. He was simply emphasizing the fact that all true teaching had to be my work.

Think with me for a moment of how instantaneously I can reveal a spiritual truth to you. Take for example the truth of the "new birth." You never understood it until I revealed it to you, and then suddenly you declared, "It is mine. I am born again. God has forgiven me. I have peace at last." As swift as a flash of lightning, the truth of the new birth was written in your understanding by me.

I have stated that one of my names is the "Spirit of truth." Does this suggest something to you? Are you aware that there is in this world a "spirit of error"? Listen to the apostle Paul's warning to young Timothy: "But the Holy Spirit tells us clearly that in the last times some in the church will turn away from Christ and become eager followers of teachers with devil-inspired ideas" (I Tim. 4:1, *TLB*). Again in Paul's second letter to the same young man, he says, "In fact, evil men and false teachers will become worse and worse, deceiving many, they themselves having been deceived by Satan" (II Tim. 3:13, *TLB*).

In writing to believers, John says, "Beloved, believe not every spirit, but try the spirits whether they are of God: because many false prophets are gone out into the world" (I John 4:1). I, the Spirit of truth, am the only One who can keep you safe from the spirit of error.

I, the Spirit of truth, am not only your teacher but, as I have already suggested, I am also your prayer partner. How often have you felt helpless in this whole matter of prayer? Prayer is communion. Prayer is intercession. Prayer is supplication. Prayer is praise. Prayer is so many things and often so difficult that you need my help. Right? That is why Paul assured the brave believers in Rome that they had a prayer partner; "Likewise the Spirit also helpeth our infirmities: for we know not what we should pray for as we ought: but the Spirit itself maketh intercession for us with groanings which cannot be uttered. And he that searcheth the hearts [Heavenly Father] knoweth what is the mind of the Spirit, because he [Spirit] maketh intercession for the saints according to the will of God" (Rom. 8:26, 27).

No less than three times in Scripture you are told to "pray in the Spirit." What does that mean? It means to pray when I tell you to. You are to be sensitive to my promptings.

The going was rough for the first little group of believers in Jerusalem. Herod the king, in order to please the people, cast the

Christians into jail and had James, the brother of John, beheaded. This brought him great applause so he determined to cut off Peter's head also. Just before Easter he jailed Peter with the intent of beheading him right after Easter.

The believers had one powerful resource—prayer. They used it and without ceasing made intercession unto God for Peter. God heard their prayer and at midnight He sent an angel to the prison to deliver Peter. The angel did a tidy piece of work. He awakened the sleeping Peter, took off his chains, unlocked the doors, led Peter out to safety, and then relocked all the doors. What saved Peter from the fate of James? Why did Peter have such a long ministry? Because a little group of believers knew what it was to "pray in the Spirit."

A lone missionary out in China grew tired and discouraged. His zeal withered and dried up. Praying became a whirl of thought that passed through his mind but never left his lips. He read the Bible as one might read a popular magazine. He preached with no inspiration. He was totally defeated and all he really wanted to do was to return home. One morning as he was sitting quietly and thinking about some excuse he might use for leaving the field, he became aware of a holy presence and he heard an inner voice say, "I will see you through. I will see you through." Doubt, fear, and defeat left him. He suddenly knew beyond the shadow of a doubt that God would see him through.

Why the sudden change from defeat to victory? The night before a lady in Pasadena, California, had been awakened with a heavy burden to pray. She tried to delay her praying until morning but she couldn't sleep. Finally she got out of bed and, with her prayer list in her hand, dropped on her knees. When she came to this particular missionary's name, all she could do was sob, "Lord, I don't know his exact need but whatever it is please see him through."

Why did the missionary spend seventeen years rather than seventeen months on mainland China? There is only one answer. A prayer partner seven thousand miles away knew how to "pray in the Spirit."

Christ by His death unlocked the door which separates man from God. "For through him [Christ] we both have access by one Spirit unto the Father" (Eph. 2:18). This means I simply open the door Christ unlocked. Christ opened the way to the Father. I give you the ability to enter. So pray and I will see that your praying is adjusted to the will of God and you in turn will experience real answers to prayer because I am your prayer partner.

41

6

Your Bible and I

Part 2

Would you believe it? You can know as much about God as you want to know. The whole thing depends upon the intensity of your desire. Because God is infinite, I never run out of information about Him to share with you. When Jesus said to His disciples, "I have yet many things to show unto you," He was looking forward to the day in which the Epistles would be written and in which I would be teaching the things of God to you.

This means that theology should be the most exciting study in all the world. No other study is as close to being infinite. The plain fact is every other "ology" is a branch (sometimes distant) of theology. This is another way of saying that you cannot fully appreciate physiology, geology, archeology, or any other "ology" without a knowledge of God (theology). Because He is the foundation and cause of everything in creation, nothing is seen in proper perspective until you have a God-given focus on theology.

Creation has a way of talking about and singing about the Creator. However, creation's testimony is limited. Furthermore, man's ears are not on a proper frequency to understand the testimony of creation distinctly. For this reason, God cannot be discovered scientifically. He is not a definition—He is a relation. And this is where I come into the picture. Intellectual acumen in itself cannot discern God. Some of the world's most knowledgeable men have been atheists and agnostics. But don't forget, their "wisdom" is foolishness in the sight of God. God's "simplicity" is far wiser than all of man's accumulated knowledge.

Wisdom comes only to the person who studies to show himself approved unto God. You can be amazingly knowledgeable and still not be wise. It is possible to accumulate several Ph.D. degrees and still lack wisdom. On the other hand, it is possible to have a limited amount of knowledge and still possess real wisdom. You doubtless know some people who have never obtained college degrees, but who are extremely wise in relation to both time and eternity.

The psalmist discovered the possibility of all of this many centuries ago. He said, "Nothing is perfect except your words. Oh, how I love them. I think about them all day long. They make me wiser than my enemies, because they are my constant guide. Yes, wiser than my teachers, for I am ever thinking of your rules. They make me even wiser than the aged" (Ps. 119:96-100, *TLB*). Sounds like a pretty good recipe for the person who wants to be wiser than his enemies, his teachers, and even his elders.

"No mere man has ever seen, heard or even imagined what wonderful things God has ready for those who love the Lord" (I Cor. 2:9, *TLB*). But it is my privilege to reveal those things to you. The following verses explain exactly what I mean: "No one can really know what anyone else is thinking, or what he is really like, except that person himself. And no one can know God's thoughts except God's own Spirit. And God has actually given us His Spirit (not the world's spirit) to tell us about the wonderful free gifts of grace and blessing that God has given us" (I Cor. 2:11, 12, *TLB*).

Interesting, isn't it, that a scientist can spend thirty years studying nothing more than the many species of frogs? If the humble frog can provide a lifetime of study for a brilliant man, then how unsearchable and past finding out are the thoughts and character of God? It is little wonder that the prophet wrote concerning Him, As the heavens are high above the earth so are his thoughts above our thoughts. It is certainly not possible for the human intellect to plumb the depths of the character of God. Obviously, one would have to be infinite in order to go to infinite depths or heights.

The love of God, the wisdom of God, the righteousness of God, and the power of God are just a few of the attributes of His nature that are unfathomable. And that is what I was talking about when I said, "You can know as much about God as you want to know." This simply means that any study of theology is inexhaustible. I will always have more and more to teach you.

Unfortunately, some people (like the early disciples) seem to be dull of hearing. This is why Paul prayed for the Ephesian believers that God would give them a spirit of wisdom and revelation in the knowledge of Christ. It was his desire for them, as it is mine for you, that "you be able to feel and understand . . . how long, how wide, how deep, and how high His love really is; and to experience this love for yourselves, though it is so great that you will never see the end of it or fully know or understand it" (Eph. 3:18, 19, *TLB*).

Have you ever heard anyone say, "I was an alcoholic and a wife-beater but my whole life and character have been changed as a result of studying a Sears Roebuck catalog"? Sounds stupid, doesn't it? The fact is men's lives are not transformed by the reading of newspapers, weekly magazines, or the writings of the philosophers. But many a man has become a "new creature" as he has read or studied Scripture. You see, the Bible is the "sword of the Spirit." It is the instrument I use to probe the hearts of people.

Though this has already been mentioned, I want to go a little farther in showing you just how important the Word of God is to you. The psalmist has glorified God's Word in this little summary: "The law of the Lord is perfect, restoring the soul; the testimony of the Lord is sure, making wise the simple. The precepts of the Lord are right, rejoicing the heart; the commandment of the Lord is pure, enlightening the eyes. The fear of the Lord is clean, enduring forever; the judgments of the Lord are true; they are righteous altogether. They are more desirable than gold, yes, than

46

much fine gold; sweeter also than honey and the drippings of the honeycomb. Moreover, by them Thy servant is warned; in keeping them there is great reward" (Ps. 19:7-11, *NASB*).

That statement certainly makes it look as if every Christian ought to be happy for the privilege of reading and studying God's Word. No wonder Paul encouraged the young people and adults in the church at Colosse to "Let the word of Christ dwell in you richly in all wisdom . . ." (Col. 3:16).

You can do this by:

1. Giving careful attention to Scripture every time you hear it taught or preached.

2. Maintaining a daily Bible reading schedule.

3. Spending some time every week digging into (studying) a Bible passage.

4. Memorizing verses, paragraphs, or chapters of God's Word.

5. Meditating on (thinking about) Bible truths. Sound good? Well, more about it in the next chapter.

THE GREATEST BOOK EVER WRITTEN

The Bible contains the mind of God, the state of man, the way of salvation, the doom of sinners, and the happiness of believers. Its doctrines are holy, its precepts binding, its histories true, and its decisions immutable. Read it to be wise, believe it to be safe, and practice it to be holy. It contains light to direct you, food to nourish you, and comfort to cheer you. It is the traveler's map, the pilgrim's staff, the pilot's compass, the soldier's sword, the Christian's charter. Here paradise is restored, heaven opened, the gates of hell disclosed. Christ is its grand subject, God's glory its end. It should fill the memory, rule the heart, and guide the feet. It is given to you in life and will be opened at the judgment. It condemns all who trifle with its sacred contents and rewards those who study and obey it.

—Author unknown

Your Bible and I

Part 3

How about letting me give you a rundown on several reasons why the Word of God ought to be very important to you?

1. You have become a child of God through His Word. John 20:31 says, "But these are written, that ye might believe that Jesus is the Christ, the Son of God; and that believing ye might have life through his name." Then Peter tells you that you are "born again not of corruptible seed [the life

49

passed on to you by your parents] but by the incorruptible [immortal] seed which is the living and abiding word of God."

2. Your growth comes through God's Word. "So then faith cometh by hearing," says Paul, "and hearing by the word of God" (Rom. 10:17). To this Peter adds, "If you have tasted the Lord's goodness and kindness, cry for more, as a baby cries for milk." Eat God's Word, read it, think about it—and grow strong in the Lord. Along with this, Paul prayed that you might go beyond the "milk stage" to the eating of the strong meat of the Word of God. I can do very little for your spiritual growth if you are careless with your Bible.

3. Cleansing comes through the Word of God. The psalmist asked the question in Psalm 119:9, "How can a young may stay pure?" His answer was, "By reading your Word and following its rules" (*TLB*). In Ephesians 5:26 you are told about the washing of the water by the Word, and Jesus, in His prayer for all believers, says, "Make them pure and holy through teaching them Your words of truth" (John 17:17, *TLB*).

4. Satisfaction and success come to you through God's Word. Did you know that the word *success* is found only once in the Bible? It is in Joshua 1:8: "This book of the law shall not depart out of thy mouth; but thou

shalt meditate therein day and night, that thou mayest observe to do according to all that is written therein: for then thou shalt make thy way prosperous, and then thou shalt have good success." This is certainly a challenging promise. You should not really need anything more to motivate you into being a diligent student of God's Word. However, there are many other verses to encourage you along this line.

Perhaps you have already memorized the first Psalm. Take a second look at the first three verses: "How blessed is the man who does not walk in the counsel of the wicked, nor stand in the path of sinners, nor sit in the seat of scoffers! But his delight is in the law of the Lord, and in His law he meditates day and night. And he will be like a tree firmly planted by streams of water, which yields its fruit in its season, and its leaf does not wither; and in whatever he does he prospers" (*NASB*). That sounds like the life "more abundant" Jesus promised to give those who trust in Him.

Those verses, along with the exhortation given to young Timothy, will help you understand why I, the Holy Spirit, am so concerned about your relationship to Scripture. "But you must keep on believing the things you have been taught. You know they are true for you know that you can trust those of us who have taught you. You know how, when you were a small child, you were taught the holy Scriptures; and it is these that make you wise to accept God's salvation by trusting in Christ Jesus. The whole Bible was given to us by inspiration from God and is useful to teach us what is true and to make us realize what is wrong in our lives; it straightens us out and helps us do what is right. It is God's way of making us well prepared at every point, fully equipped to do good to everyone" (II Tim. 3:14-17, *TLB*).

5. Direction is another of the wonderful things you obtain through the Word of God. Again and again in the Old Testament you will find my ministry in the lives of God's servants expressed in such words as "and the Word of the Lord came unto. . . ." You will recall that Jeremiah responded to such an experience by saying, "Thy words were found, and I did eat them; and thy word was unto me the joy and rejoicing of mine heart" (15:16).

You have already been reminded of God's blessing upon some of the Old Testament prophets when they walked according to my instructions. I told Israel exactly what to do in order to conquer the powerful walled city of Jericho. They did it and the walls of that great city fell. Immediately following this, the armies of Israel were humiliated by the people in the little city of Ai. Israel's defeat was the result of her disobedience to my commands.

You walk "in the light" only when you follow the instructions of God's Word. The psalmist expressed it this way: "Your words are a flashlight to light the path ahead of me, and keep me from stumbling" (Ps. 119:105, *TLB*). Perhaps you have already discovered that when you are faithful in Bible study and obedient to the principles found therein, you do walk in the light and you do not stumble.

As your instructor in the things of God, I, the Holy Spirit, am deeply concerned that all five of the things mentioned above should become important realities to you. I delight to take the things of Christ and share them with you. All I need to do this is your time and willingness to expose yourself to God's Word. Perhaps you should make up your mind to be like the Bereans. Of them it is written, "Now these were more noble-minded than those in Thessalonica, for they received the word with great eagerness, examining the Scriptures daily, to see whether these things were so. Many of them therefore believed, along with a number of prominent Greek women and men" (Acts 17:11, 12, *NASB*).

Searching Scripture daily is both a beautiful and a needful habit. Try it! You can do it! "Do you want more and more of God's kindness and peace? Then learn to know Him better and better. For as you know Him better, He will give you, through His great power, everything you need for living a truly good life: He even shares His own glory and His own goodness with us! And by that same mighty power He has given us all the other rich and wonderful blessings He promised; for instance, the promise to save us from the lust and rottenness all around us, and to give us His own character" (II Peter 1:2-4, *TLB*).

"His own character"—yes, that expresses exactly what my desire is for your life. I want you to be conformed to the image of Jesus, and I can accomplish that if you will only let me. You will remember that though John the Baptist did no miracles, his life and character made people feel he might be the Christ. Your Bible tells you he was a Spirit-filled man. Your life, too, will be Christlike when it is filled with God's Word and when I am in control.

Your Business and I

Part 1

By "business" I refer to the way in which you invest your life and how you use your time, training, and talents. As a twelve-year-old, Jesus said, "I must be about my Father's business." If that is an expression of your desire, the following chapters will be of special help to you.

Not only am I . . . God the Holy Spirit . . . in you, but you are in God. I know that seems impossible though it sounds wonderfully secure. Well, it is true and it is possible though my work. The Bible says, "But the Holy Spirit has fitted us all together into one body. We have been baptized into Christ's body by the one Spirit, and have all been given that same Holy Spirit" (I Cor. 12:13, *TLB*). If that sounds a little confusing to you, just hold on a minute.

On the day I brought you to the place of conversion through my probing, convicting work, I also made you a member of the body of Christ. And all members of the body of Christ are joined to the Head, who is Christ. As in the physical body all the trillions of cells are held together by an intercellular substance, even so I hold all the cells of Christ's body together. The cells of the human body differ but they all have the same life. The cells of the body of Christ differ but they all have the same divine life—my life.

For true health and greatest efficiency each cell must do its part. No cell can fight against any other cell. Each cell or each member must cooperate with each other member. Failure of any one member causes injury to all the members. If you snag your finger on a rusty nail and fail to do anything about it, more than likely blood poisoning will set in. This will poison your entire blood stream so that not just the finger but the whole body will suffer. Just so, as a Christian if you allow impurity in your life, you weaken the testimony and the effectiveness of the whole body of Christ.

You might argue that what you do is your own business, but after you become a member of the body of Christ you no longer live unto yourself. Have you read that sad little story about the young man in the church at Corinth who was sleeping with his stepmother? That's right. He was cheating on his own father and committing adultery with his father's second wife. Here was a believer living in sin that even unbelievers didn't condone. His conduct brought disgrace to the whole church and discredit to the name of Christ.

I have placed you in the body of Christ exactly where I want you. Furthermore, I have given you a special gift to enable you to accomplish the work I have planned for you. To understand this more clearly, look again at the physical body. Note how perfectly every part of the body is placed, the feet where they can walk, the hands where they can grasp, the eyes where they can see, etc. Just so, in the body of Christ you have been rightly placed for the good of the whole body.

"For as the body is one, and hath many members, and all the members of that one body, being many, are one body: so also is Christ . . . For the body is not one member, but many. If the foot shall say, Because I am not the hand, I am not of the body; is it therefore not of the body?" (I Cor. 12:12, 14, 15).

Of course it is part of the body. It just possesses an inferiority complex. It thinks it is unimportant. How foolish! After all, how would you get around without feet? If the ear should call a strike and complain that because it is not the eye it is not of the body, is it therefore not of the body? If the whole body were an eye, where would the hearing be? There is no room for an inferiority complex, for I have placed you in the "body" just where I want you and have given you a spiritual gift which makes your life and work for God possible.

And, remember, the eye cannot say to the hand, "I have no need of you." There is, in other words, no room for a superiority complex. The hand does a different job but it is just as needed as the eye. So in the body of Christ there is no room for divisions or jealousy.

The apostle Paul claims to use two of my gifts. He says he is an evangelist and a teacher. Read his wonderful sermon given on Mars Hill and you see the "gift of preaching" at work (Acts 17:22-31). Listen to his defense before King Agrippa. He states that God has saved him "To open their (Gentiles') eyes, and to turn them from darkness to light, and from the power of Satan unto God, that they may receive forgiveness of sins, and inheritance among them which are sanctified by faith that is in me" (Acts 26:18). Again you see the evangelist and preacher. Then take any of his letters (called epistles) and read them carefully. While reading, you will become aware that he really has the gift of teaching. I gave Paul all his gifts. I give to every believer the gift, or gifts, necessary to do the work God has for him.

Your problem may not be the lack of a gift but failure to discover what gift I have given you. Neglect of this important truth hinders the body of Christ and embarrasses me. If you bought and wrapped a beautiful gift for a dear friend only to discover that three months or three years after you delivered the gift your friend still had not troubled to open it, how would you feel? Believe me, I am grieved when God's people neglect my gifts to them.

Your Business and I

Part 2

As I have already said, I give to everyone the gift *or gifts* necessary to enable him to do the work I want him to do. I usually start by giving a believer one gift, but I am generous. If a person needs another gift due to fresh responsibilities, I give him what he needs. If you require more than one gift in order to fulfill God's purpose, I will give it to you.

Let me illustrate this by telling you about Philip. He was a member of the fast-growing church in Jerusalem. He had the privilege of daily listening to the stimulating teaching of the apostles. He rejoiced in the growing church but apparently was not too involved in any work.

The people of the church liked him because of his excellent character. Scripture says he was a man of "good reputation, full of the Spirit and of wisdom" (Acts 6:3, *NASB*). Who wouldn't like that kind of man? When I placed him in the body of Christ I gave him the gift of "administration," but until a crisis arose in the church he didn't use his gift too much.

However, the church was growing so fast that the apostles soon discovered they could not keep up with the work. They were attempting to teach the multitude of new believers and at the same time do the daily work of caring for the many widows. They soon realized they had to stick to priorities and said to the members of the church, "It is not desirable for us to neglect the word of God in order to serve tables. But select from among you, brethren, seven men of good reputation, full of the Spirit and of wisdom, whom we may put in charge of this task. But we will devote ourselves to prayer, and to the ministry of the word" (Acts 6:2-4, *NASB*).

The congregation did as the apostles suggested and Philip became one of the first seven deacons. In this work of caring for the widows, he had ample opportunity to use the gift of administration I had given him. Things went well until a zealous young Pharisee named Saul tried to wipe out the church. Saul's revolution was so successful that it played havoc with the congregation. Some members were caught and beaten, others were thrown into jail, and many fled for their lives.

Knowing he would have to leave home, Philip prayed that God would show him what to do so his time would really count. That prayer was answered as I led him to Samaria. The Samaritans were idolaters and knew little about Jesus Christ and His church. As this was Philip's new world, it was his responsibility to share his faith was the Samaritans. For this work he needed something more than the gift of "administration," so I immediately gave him the gift of "evangelism," and "Philip . . . began proclaiming Christ to them" (Acts 8:5, *NASB*).

The people were impressed but needed more evidence that what Philip said was true, so I gave him the gift of "healing." Now the Samaritans not only heard but they saw. Right before their eyes the paralyzed were made whole, the lame were healed, and those with unclean spirits were delivered. As a result many were saved and there was great joy in the city.

Now you can see how lavish I am in giving gifts to enable anyone to fulfill the ministry I have for him. Philip's first gift was *administration;* his second, *evangelism;* and his third, *healing.* But that is not all. In an entirely different circumstance I gave him still another gift.

One day I told Philip to pick up and leave the harvest of souls in Samaria and travel down a desert road toward the city of Gaza. The order didn't exactly make sense to Philip, but with unquestioning obedience he took off. One of the first people he came across on this desolate road was the treasurer of Ethiopia. This eunuch had traveled all the way from Ethiopia to Jerusalem to worship. He was convinced the gods of Ethiopia could do him no good. Maybe, he thought, he would find new light in Jerusalem. He received very little help from the priests in the Holy City, but he was able to purchase a portion of the Old Testament. While he was riding the long road home in his chariot, he read from the book of Isaiah. And I said to Philip, "Go up and join this chariot." Philip hurried to the side of the beautiful chariot and asked, "Do you understand what you are reading?" The treasurer responded, "Well, how could I, unless someone guides me?" (Acts 8:30, 31, *NASB*).

Then in a real turn of events he stopped his

chariot and asked Philip to join him and teach him what the prophet Isaiah was talking about. Philip now found himself in a place where he had to expound the meaning of a very difficult passage in the Old Testament. I immediately gave Philip the gift of "teaching." This gift enabled Philip to clearly prove to the eunuch that Isaiah was talking about Jesus. So convincingly was the passage explained to the treasurer that he believed on Jesus and was baptized, and he in turn carried the good news into North Africa.

Do you see from Philip's experiences that I am lavish in my giving of spiritual gifts? Philip started with *one* and ended up with *four*. Had he needed more, I would have given them to him.

And what about you? I have given you a gift. Discover what it is and use it for Christ's glory. I assure you that when you are put into a ministry in which you need other gifts I will give them to you.

Your Business and I

Part 3

Perhaps you need help in discovering what my gift to you is. The following analogy should assist you in finding the answer.

In what trade are these men involved: carpenters, bricklayers, plumbers, electricians, and painters? You are right—the building trade.

You may not be an expert builder, but you are observant enough to know that the tools used by a carpenter differ from those used by a painter. Those used by a plumber differ from those used by an electrician. In the building trade each man has a particular job to do and his job requires special tools. You can't pound nails with a paintbrush or lay bricks with a plumber's wrench. The important thing is that buildings are built when all of these men use their tools to the best of their ability to do the job.

That is exactly the way it is in the church. As the master builder, I am building a temple for God. Jesus Christ is the foundation of that temple, and its walls are built of living stones. I know where and how each Christian can make his biggest contribution to the erecting of the temple. I know, for example, whether a man would be a better bricklayer than an electrician or a better plumber than a carpenter. I own the tools and I am in a good position to give him the right ones for his job.

But before going farther, let's take a look at those tools as they are listed in I Corinthians 12:7-11, "The Holy Spirit displays God's power through each of us as a means of helping the entire church. To one person the Spirit gives the ability to give wise advice; someone else may be especially good at studying and teaching, and this is his gift from the same Spirit. He gives special faith to another, and to someone else the power to heal the sick. He gives power for doing miracles to some, and to others power to prophesy and preach. He gives someone else the power to know whether evil spirits are speaking through those who claim to be giving God's messages—or whether it is really the Spirit of God who is speaking. Still another person is able to speak in languages he never learned; and others, who do not know the language either, are given power to understand what he is saying. It is the same and only Holy Spirit who gives all these gifts and powers, deciding which each one of us should have" (*TLB*).

Please note that I am the one who decides which tool each worker should use. I know how you can make your biggest contribution in the building of God's temple. I'll have more to say about that later on. In the meantime, think carefully about this passage from God's Word: "God has given each of us the ability to do certain things well. So if God has given you the ability to prophesy, then prophesy whenever you can—as often as your faith is strong enough to receive a message from God. If your gift is that of serving others, serve them well. If you are a teacher, do a good job of teaching. If you are a preacher, see to it that your sermons are strong and helpful. If God has given you money, be generous in helping others with it. If God has given you administrative ability and put you in charge of the work of others, take the responsibility seriously. Those who offer comfort to the sorrowing should do so with Christian cheer" (Rom. 12:6-8, *TLB*).

Now just one more passage. I refer to Ephesians 4:11-13: "Some of us have been given special ability as apostles; to others He has given the gift of being able to preach well; some have special ability in winning people to Christ, helping them to trust Him as their Savior; still others have a gift for caring for God's people as a shepherd does his sheep, leading and teaching them in the ways of God. Why is it that He gives us these special abilities to do certain things best? It is that God's people will be equipped to do better work for Him, building up the church, the body of Christ, to a position of strength and maturity; Until finally we all believe alike about our salvation and about our Savior, God's Son, and all become full-grown in the Lord—yes, to the point of being filled full with Christ" (*TLB*).

These passages are pretty conclusive, aren't they? They teach that I am the master builder and that I hand out the tools to the workmen. Actually, no one else is in a position to do this. I see the whole blueprint in a way that no mere man could see it. I know to whom to give the tools and I know exactly where the job needs to be done.

An Old Testament illustration will help you

see this more clearly. The children of Israel were instructed to build a tabernacle. It was the place in which they were to meet with God. They were to build the tabernacle according to the specific instructions I gave them. Note Exodus 31:1-6: "The Lord also said to Moses, 'See, I have appointed Bezalel . . . and have filled him with the Spirit of God, giving him great wisdom, ability, and skill in constructing the Tabernacle and everything it contains. He is highly capable as an artistic designer of objects made of gold, silver, and bronze. He is skilled, too, as a jeweler and in carving wood. And I have appointed Oholiab . . . to be his assistant; moreover, I have given special skill to all who are known as experts, so that they can make all the things I have instructed you to make'" (*TLB*).

Like the tabernacle in the wilderness and Solomon's temple in Jerusalem, the church of Jesus Christ is being built by those I have chosen and equipped for the job. And you are part of the work force.

Paul referred to himself as a master builder and he warned each believer to be careful how he built. He said it was possible to build with such perishable things as wood, hay, and stubble or to build with lasting things like gold, silver, and precious stones. It was obviously

his desire that each builder should build with
eternity's values in view.

But I still haven't really answered your
question as to how you may know what my
gift is to you. Perhaps the most practical way
for you to discover it is to become involved in
my program of soul-winning and church-
edifying.

An apprentice in any trade soon discovers
that there are one or more fields in which he
is particularly adept. He then specializes in
that field. As you become involved in the
service of the Lord Jesus Christ, you will find
that there is some area in which you can make
some special contribution to God's program.
You may discover God has entrusted to you
musical ability that can be used for His glory.
Or as the result of teaching a Sunday school
class, it may become plain that I have given
you the ability to interestingly open God's
Word to people. It may be that Christian
hospitality or a compassion for the sick or
elderly will provide avenues of service for
you. It is possible that my biggest ministry
through you will be to children or young
people.

Now let's think again of the human body as
an analogy of the church. You, of course, had
nothing to say about the formation of your
own body. You didn't choose the color of

your hair, the length of your nose, or the size of your feet. Furthermore, you had no part in designating the number or location of the organs of your body. Your whole wonderful body was designed by God. As a perfect designer, He knew exactly what organs you needed and where to place them. The fact is you would have probably been a nonfunctional monstrosity if it had been left to you to place the organs where you wanted them.

The same kind of divisive monstrosity appears in the body of Christ when its members begin demanding their own rights. If they decide to act as independent organs or to choose their own tools (gifts) and to use them where and how they like, they end up with that which is not according to my plan.

If you would take the time to study the makeup of your body, you would be amazed by the perfect coordination of its organs. You have probably just taken for granted much of the relationship between your eyes and ears, your brain and hands, your lungs and heart, and your nerves and skin. You probably go for days without ever thinking of your liver, gall bladder, spleen, or stomach. And, yet, each of these organs is silently and efficiently carrying on wonderful ministries for your body every day. No organ is jealous of the other and each contributes to the welfare of all the rest. If the body is going to be healthy and functional, this has to be true.

And it has to be just as true in the body of Christ. Obviously, some organs of the body are more visible than others. But this does not mean they are more important. Though the eye is a visible and important member, it is no more important than the heart or the lungs. This suggests that you must not be too concerned about a visible ministry. You should simply rejoice in the fact that you are a member of the "body," whether seen or unseen, large or small.

The all-important thing is for each member to be faithful to its particular responsibility. The "body" needs faithful transportation by those who are the feet, faithful communication by those who are the lips, faithful perception by those who are the eyes, faithful interpretation by those who are the mind, and faithful "this-and-that" by those who are "this-and-that."

How many of the following names ring a bell with you: Eprenetus, Adronicus, Junias, Urbanus, Apelles, and Aristobulus? You may not be able to place any of them. And yet they were important enough for me to record their names in the Bible. They were people, chosen and gifted by me, to make their respective contributions to the body of Christ. You see, you don't have to be a world famous evangelist or Bible teacher to be important to me. It is simply my desire that you should be yielding and obedient to me. I will then make your life the rich blessing it should be to your fellow Christians and to the world.

11

Your Behavior and I

Part 1

How would you like to have Elijah, John, or Paul spend six months in your home? Would the presence of any of them curb your life style? Are there a few changes you would want to make in your attitudes, conversation, or actions before they moved in on you? Then, perhaps you ought to take some second thoughts about the fact that your body is my home. As the Holy Spirit, I am concerned

74

about the places in which I make my home. Clean rooms are important to me.

This is another way of saying that I am vitally interested in every aspect of your life: body, soul, and spirit. Of Jesus it was said, "And Jesus increased in wisdom and stature, and in favour with God and man" (Luke 2:52). This is the kind of thing I'm interested in for you. Your mental (wisdom), physical (stature), spiritual (in favor with God), and social (and man) well-being are of concern to me. You make a serious mistake, therefore, when you departmentalize your life and leave room for me only in the realm of that which you look upon as being religious or spiritual.

You are probably aware that I have set up guidelines all through the Bible to help you in each of the above-mentioned aspects of your life. For example, "Thou shalt not have any other gods before me" relates to your spiritual well-being. "Thou shalt not steal" is tied closely to your social well-being. "Thou shalt not commit adultery" cannot be separated from your physical life. "Thou shalt not covet" has a close relationship to your thought life. Of course, these are only a few of the very broad principles. Much detailed instruction is given to you in the Bible with reference to your behavior patterns.

Perhaps you're the kind of person who has a tendency to rebel against laws, rules, or guidelines. You may have even found some Scripture verses which would tend to suggest that as a Christian you are free to forget all laws and live as you like. But don't forget that any such passages have to be understood in the light of their context. It is true that you are not bound to the ceremonial laws of the Old Testament. On the other hand, you have not been set free to break the moral laws.

Maybe you are living according to a wrong understanding of the word "freedom." A dictionary definition of freedom is "the absence of hindrance, restraint, confinement, or repression." Such a definition is terribly inadequate. Actually, freedom is "a condition or situation defined by boundaries (rules) in which a person or thing can fulfill the purpose for which it is designed."

A fish is only free to fulfill the purpose for which it is designed when it is in water. Take it outside of the boundaries of H_2O and it dies. A train is free to fulfill the purpose for which it is designed when it stays within the boundaries of its tracks. Automobiles are free to transport people safely from one place to another (the purpose for which they are designed) when rules of the road are obeyed. Even the freedom of a football player to play a good game depends upon his obedience to the rules.

Have you ever thought of the "thou shalt

not's" in a game of football? Here are a few:

1. Thou shalt not move forward before the ball is snapped.
2. Thou shalt not rough the kicker.
3. Thou shalt not hold an opposing player.
4. Thou shalt not clip an opponent.
5. Thou shalt not grab his face mask.
6. Thou shalt not interfere with a pass receiver or pass defender.
7. Thou shalt not intentionally ground the ball.
8. Thou shalt not pass to an ineligible receiver.
9. Thou shalt not step on or cross the sidelines.
10. Thou shalt not manifest unsportsmanlike conduct.

If all those rules sound negative and restrictive, then please remember that football would not be the exciting game it is without them. If every player could do that which was right in his own eyes, the game would be bedlam. Admittedly, that is only the negative side of the matter. The positive aspect provides all kinds of liberties and freedoms which make football a challenge both to the athlete and to the observer. If a thing no more important than a football game is exciting because it has guidelines, then certainly the more serious things of life need them.

You are living in a day when there are those who say, "I want to do my thing." They think doing their thing is real freedom. But this is not true. You are only really free when you are fulfilling the purpose for which you are designed. That purpose is expressed in these words, "Thou shalt love the Lord thy God with all thy heart, and with all thy soul, and with all thy strength, and with all thy mind; and thy neighbour as thyself" (Luke 10:27). This statement is simply another way of expressing the Ten Commandments from a positive angle. You are only really doing "His thing" when you are living in the light of this truth. As someone has said, "Freedom is not the liberty to do what you want. It is the power to do what you ought." And that is worth memorizing.

A test of your moral freedom is not your ability to start something. It is your ability to stop it. Anyone can start evil thoughts, actions, or conversations. It is another thing to terminate them. The Bible says that the man who commits sin is a servant of sin. Romans 6:16-18 says, "Don't you realize that you can choose your own master? You can choose sin (with death) or else obedience (with acquittal). The one to whom you offer yourself—he will take you and be your master and you will be his slave. Thank God that though you once chose to be slaves of sin, now you have obeyed with all your heart the teaching to which God has committed you. And now you are free from your old master, sin; and you have become slaves to your new master, righteousness" (TLB).

12

Your Behavior and I

Part 2

Your answers to the following questions will help you bring your life into proper perspective. First, how does your behavior affect God? Pretty important question, isn't it? The Bible says, "Anyone who says he is a Christian should live as Christ did" (I John 2:6, *TLB*). It also says that whether you "eat, or drink, or whatsoever you do, do all to the glory of God" (I Cor. 10:31).

Paul expressed his desire to live positively

for the glory of God in these words, "For to me to live is Christ" (Phil. 1:21). You are not to measure your behavior patterns by society but by your relationship with God and by the fact that your body is my temple.

Second, how does your behavior affect your fellow Christians? You have already discovered that you have the privilege and responsibility of edifying (building up) those who are your brothers and sisters in Christ. This is done not only by your spoken words but also through your manner of life. Romans 14:13 pleads with you, "Try instead to live in such a way that you will never make your brother stumble by letting him see you doing something he thinks is wrong" (*TLB*).

The apostle Paul had a good attitude in this regard. He refused to do anything he felt might offend a weaker brother. He knew there were some things that were perfectly legal for him to do. He refused to do them, however, if they would cause someone else to stumble. Though he felt there was nothing wrong in eating meat offered to idols, he was willing to forego the privilege in order to be of help to others. He said, "Don't think only of yourself. Try to think of the other fellow, too, and what is best for him" (I Cor. 10: 24, *TLB*).

And you can be sure there would be a lot less misunderstanding between Christians if they all lived according to the following guidelines: "Don't undo the work of God for a chunk of meat. Remember, there is nothing wrong with the meat, but it is wrong to eat it if it makes another stumble. The right thing to do is to quit eating meat or drinking wine or doing anything else that offends your brother or makes him sin. You may know that there is nothing wrong with what you do, even from God's point of view, but keep it to yourself; don't flaunt your faith in front of others who might be hurt by it. In this situation, happy is the man who does not sin by doing what he knows is right" (Rom. 14:20-22, *TLB*).

Third, how does your behavior affect your unbelieving friends and neighbors? When Jesus talked about the lives of believers being the salt of the earth and the light of the world, He was talking about behavior patterns that would tend to direct the minds of people toward God.

Salt is a preventative. It checks the progress of corruption. It speaks of the negative (thou shalt not) influence of Christianity. Light is the positive testimony. It shows the way. It give life. It brightens things up. With my help you can be both "salt" and "light" to your unsaved friends.

There should be something about your actions that would indicate your citizenship is in heaven. It is not just your preaching, but also your practicing which should reveal your "other worldliness." You are not to be a stumbling block to anyone, "whether they are Jews or Gentiles or Christians" (I Cor. 10:32, *TLB*).

Lastly, how does your behavior affect you? In answering this question you ought to first consider what it does to your mind. "As a man thinketh," says Scripture, "so is he." Because thoughts often produce actions, and actions habits, and habits character, it is important for you to guard your thoughts with all diligence. Any form of behavior that tends to defile your mind is dangerous to you and contrary to my will for you.

Here is some good instruction from Philippians 4:8, "Fix your thoughts on what is true and good and right. Think about things that are pure and lovely, and dwell on the fine, good things in others. Think about all you can praise God for and be glad about" (*TLB*).

Your eyes and ears are the basic avenues through which your mind is fed. How very important it is, therefore, for you to be selective in regard to the things you listen to, read, and watch.

There are forms of behavior which can have serious detrimental effects on your body. Illicit sex, drugs, liquor, nicotine, and gluttony all leave physical and moral scars. Emotional and social scars also often accompany these things. If a man sows to the flesh, he will of the flesh reap corruption.

Like Samson, you can choose to do your own thing and forget the will of God and live a defeated life without a testimony for Christ. Like Achan, you can covet material gain to the loss of spiritual values. Like David, you can yield to the lust of the flesh and suffer terrible chastisement. Or like Joseph, you can live a clean and godly life that will stand as a vibrant testimony for Christ.

With my help, you can do this even in a godless world. You can do it because your body is my temple. I dwell in you to enable you to discern between the clean and the unclean, the holy and the unholy. If you walk according to my dictates, you will fulfill the righteousness of the law and you will enjoy a peace which passes all understanding. You will be "more than conquerer" through Christ who loves you.

This is not to suggest that you will live a sinless life. There will be times when you will grieve me by your thoughts or actions. But you will be forgiven, and fellowship will be restored when you seek forgiveness.

Please make no mistake about it—I'm glad your body is my dwelling place. I love you with infinite love. I not only want to use you for Christ's glory but I am "jealous" for your best good.

Your Boldness and I

"Boldness? I'm the biggest chicken on earth. I don't have the courage to witness for Christ even when it seems as though God has tossed the ball right in my lap. I can talk to my friends about any other subject but when it comes to the gospel I clam up."

If that is an honest expression of your experience, then you need help, and I have it for you. And, incidentally, don't think you are the only one with such a problem. You have lots of company. There are many Christians who seem to be tongue-tied when it comes to testifying for Jesus. Furthermore, this is an affliction God's people have suffered with ever since the beginning of the church.

You will recall Peter's sad experience. Though he seemed to be a bold, outspoken disciple, he failed miserably when the chips were down. He would speak up when surrounded by fellow Christians, but he denied Christ three times when he was faced with unbelievers. Perhaps that jibes with your experience.

Well, don't give up! Do you remember what I did for Peter? On a day called Pentecost I filled his life, and from then on Peter became a bold witness for Christ. It took courage for him to speak to the thousands who heard him that day in Jerusalem. He boldly told them that they had nailed to the cross the Lord of glory. He claimed that God had raised from the dead "this Jesus whom you crucified." And don't think for one moment that there weren't mockers and scoffers in the audience.

It took courage for Peter to stand before the scribes, the Pharisees, and the high priest (Acts 4:11, 12) and say, "Jesus is the Messiah, a stone discarded by the builders . . . There is salvation in no one else . . . " Then when Peter was told by the religious authorities to stop all his preaching and teaching, it took courage for him to reply, "You decide whether God

85

wants us to obey you instead of Him! We cannot stop telling about the wonderful things we saw Jesus do and heard Him say" (Acts 4:19, 20, *TLB*). All of Peter's boldness can be explained by my presence in his life.

Stephen is another man whose witness for Christ demonstrates spiritual courage. He was not an apostle—he was a layman. He did not have the privilege of associating with Jesus for three years. He was converted after Jesus had ascended to heaven. He never had the privilege of going to a Bible school. But it is said of him that he was "full of faith and of the Holy Spirit." Those who opposed him and finally killed him could not stand up to the "wisdom and the Spirit" with which he spoke.

All of this is a way of reminding you that you cannot enjoy boldness or courage in your witness for Jesus apart from my presence in your life. Of me it has been written, "For the Holy Spirit, God's gift, does not want you to be afraid of people, but to be wise and strong, and to love them and enjoy being with them" (II Tim. 1:7, *TLB*). I am the Spirit of power, of love, and of a disciplined mind.

And here are a couple of practical suggestions. First, reject the spirit of fear. You may or may not be timid by nature. Whichever the case, you can be certain that the spirit of fear comes from Satan. He does not want you to talk about Jesus.

Second, join the early believers in their prayer for boldness. After being threatened by the rulers of the Jews, they prayed, "And now, O Lord, hear their threats, and grant to your servants great boldness in their preaching" (Acts 4:29, *TLB*). That prayer was answered and the believers were "filled with the Holy Spirit and boldly preached God's message" (Acts 4:31, *TLB*). That is pretty plain, isn't it? You can't separate a courageous testimony for Christ from my presence and work in and through you. And I am no "respecter of persons." I am just as ready to give you boldness as I was to make Peter a fearless witness. Why don't you accept this fact in quiet faith right now and thank God for it?

My greatest delight is to testify of Jesus, but I can only do it through you. You see, your body is my place of habitation. Your feet provide for me a method of transportation and your lips a means of communication. I speak to human ears through human lips. If you will think your way through the Book of Acts, you will soon discover that every conversion resulted from my ministry in the hearts of unbelievers through the hearts of believers. This should make you realize how important you are to me. My greatest desire is to reveal God's love to someone else through you. You are the channel through which the grace of God is conveyed to lonely people.

Before you were converted, you allowed your lips to express all kinds of thoughts, ideas, and desires. Some of them were displeasing to me. Your conversation was a witness to the fact that you belonged to the world. Now that you are a child of God, your life and lips should bear testimony to the fact that you love Jesus Christ. When love is real it seems to find ways of expressing itself, whether it is love for God or for people.

Paul felt the business of being a witness for Christ was both important and exciting. He was firmly convinced that it was his responsibility to share the greatest message in the world with as many people as possible. In fact, he felt the message of God's love was so great that it just had to be told to everyone. He looked upon himself as a debtor. God had done so much for him and was willing to do so much for others that Paul had a burning desire to witness to both civilized peoples and heathen nations.

In II Corinthians 5:19, 20 (*TLB*), Paul says, "For God was in Christ, restoring the world to Himself, no longer counting men's sins against them but blotting them out. This is the wonderful message He has given us to tell others. We are Christ's ambassadors. God is using us to speak to you: we beg you, as though Christ Himself were here pleading with you, receive the love He offers you—be reconciled to God." Isn't that great! Paul knew he was an authoritative mouthpiece (on the high level of an ambassador) for God. What a privilege! God's ambassador! Yes, that is exactly what the Bible says you are.

You are a citizen of heaven living on earth. It is your responsibility to tell earth's citizens about heaven's love for them. The message you are to share is the "good news." Perhaps your friends and neighbors are more hungry for that good news than you have realized. At any rate, they must be given the opportunity to hear and receive it or they will go to a Godless eternity.

If you will trust and obey, I will give you the boldness you need to witness for Christ. Let's get on with the job! You will grow in your spiritual experience, others will be brought to Christ, and God will be glorified. You can't ask for more than that.

14

Your Beauty and I

Flowers and trees are beautiful. Mountains, rivers, lakes, and even deserts are beautiful. But certainly not people! Of course people are beautiful. God never created anything more beautiful than people. Not that all people are physically attractive. But what is so earth-shaking about that? True beauty is deeper than skin.

King David expressed the thing I am talking about when he said, "And let the beauty of the Lord our God be upon us" (Ps. 90:17). It was David's desire to dwell in the house of the

Lord all the days of his life in order that he might continually "behold the beauty of the Lord" (Ps. 27:4).

If you will study the life of Jesus carefully, you will see how beautiful His character was. In fact, you won't find anything else like it in all of history. He was the exemplification of all that is suggested by the phrase "the fruit of the Spirit." And the wonderful thing is He has made provision for His own qualities of character to become a part of your experience.

Stephen was made of the same flesh and blood you are. But he became a man "full of faith and of the Holy Spirit." Those who watched him while he was on trial for his life "saw his face as it had been the face of an angel" (Acts 6:15). While being stoned to death, he cried out, "Lord, lay not this sin to their charge" (Acts 7:60). Sounds like he had obtained some of his Lord's character, doesn't it?

And listen to this description of Simeon, "He was a good man, very devout, filled with the Holy Spirit and constantly expecting the Messiah to come soon" (Luke 2:25, *TLB*). Almost the same thing is said about Barnabas: "Barnabas was a kindly person, full of the Holy Spirit and strong in faith" (Acts 11:24, *TLB*). John the Baptist was so much like

Jesus that some people thought he must be the Messiah.

I am not suggesting that any of these men were perfect. They had their battles with their carnal nature just like you do. But they lived in close fellowship with Jesus Christ and became fruitful. Let me expand on that thought.

In John 15, Jesus says, "I am the vine; you are the branches." The vine and the branch have to do with fruit bearing. Carrying that metaphor a little farther, let me add that I am the life-bearing "substance" that produces the fruit. For this reason Scripture does not speak of the fruit of the Christian but "the fruit of the Spirit." "But the fruit of the Spirit is love, joy, peace, longsuffering, gentleness, goodness, faith, meekness, temperance" (Gal. 5:22, 23). Put all those qualities into one person and he becomes beautiful in any man's language.

Let's look at that piece by piece.

LOVE. The object of true love is a loving God and His unloving creatures. To enable you to know whether you have the real thing or just a poor imitation, let me show you the character of my love as it is given in I Corinthians 13:4, 5. My love is very patient. It is kind and never jealous or envious. The love I give is never boastful, proud, or arrogant. It does not act unbecomingly and is never selfish or rude. Even in difficult circumstances it does not get irritable or touchy. It refuses to become provoked. My love really has character. You are capable in your own strength of producing only an easily-spotted counterfeit of such love, so why don't you drop yours and take mine?

In I Corinthians 13:6-8, you find a picture of love's daily habits. I said daily because my love is constant. It does not have its high days and its low days. It is always the same. My love does not hold a grudge and will hardly even notice when others do it wrong. It is never glad about injustice and does not rejoice in unrighteousness, but it does rejoice when truth wins out.

Is this the quality of your love for Jesus and mankind? If you love Jesus with my love, you will be loyal to Him no matter what it costs. You will always believe in Him and at all times expect the best of Him. You will always stand your ground in defending Him. Human love is fickle, whereas my love is the kind of which martyrs are made. Why not accept this wonderful truth now, "for we know how dearly God loves us, and we feel this warm love everywhere within us because God has given us the Holy Spirit to fill our hearts with His love" (Rom 5:5, *TLB*)?

JOY. I am not speaking of a happiness that has its roots in happenstances. I mean a joy in

God . . . a joy in the fact that you have His life, which is eternal life . . . a joy one experiences in the peace of a clear conscience . . . a joy even in being counted worthy to suffer razzing and misunderstanding for Jesus' sake. Though He knew His followers would face many obstacles and much opposition, Jesus said He wanted His joy to be in them and He wanted their joy to be full (John 15:11). That's the kind of supernatural joy I give.

PEACE. My peace is the kind that fills the heart when circumstances call for fear. The apostle Peter was imprisoned one night and was to be beheaded the next morning. The anticipation of such a cruel fate would normally keep one awake all night. But Scripture testifies, "and Peter slept." That's the deep quality of peace I produce. It "isn't fragile like the peace the world gives." Are things in your heart, your home, your school nerve-wracking? How about claiming my peace? You cannot comprehend it, but you can experience it (Phil. 4:7).

LONGSUFFERING. Let me talk about Peter again. You remember that he left his fishing business and walked with Jesus for three years. Once when Jesus asked His disciples who they thought He was, Peter boldly declared, "Thou are the Christ." Peter really knew. Yet when Peter was among Jesus' enemies and the opportunity came to acknowledge Christ as his Savior and friend, he flunked the test and three times denied he even knew Jesus. And how did Jesus react in the face of such betrayal? He just turned and looked at Peter. That is the kind of long-suffering I give. You can't begin to match it, can you? Then, why don't you drop yours and take mine?

KINDNESS. How considerate are you of the needs of others? When Jesus saw a crowd that had gone all day without food, He cared. His disciples didn't. They said, "Send them away." The disciples didn't want to be bothered by the needs of others. Are you that way? If you are, I can change all that. I can make you considerate of others, helpful to the handicapped, and kind to the underdog, the disliked, the elderly, and the timid.

GOODNESS. Do you have a brother or a sister? If you don't, you do have a mother and dad. You also have teachers and fellow students. You have ordinary friends and real special friends. As they watch your life, are they impressed by your goodness? Or is yours the natural kind that under its breath says, "If you will be good to me I will be good to you"? Do you go out of your way to be good to someone?

Do you recall the funeral Jesus saw coming out of the city gate? The one in the casket was the only son of an anguished widow. He was her only hope and now that hope was being buried. Jesus was terribly busy but not too busy to express His concern and goodness. He stopped the funeral procession, put His hand on the casket, and ordered the young man to rise from the dead. He then gave the boy back to his mother. Her hope was no longer dead but alive because Jesus was good and cared about the needs and feelings of others.

You, of course, aren't called upon to raise the dead. But do you realize that by thoughtfulness and goodness you can raise hopes and lift the spirits of those around you? That's the kind of goodness I will give you as soon as you get rid of your superficial kind.

FAITH. The apostle Paul was caught in a fierce storm at sea. He wasn't alone. There were 275 others on the ship. Things were real bad. The captain couldn't navigate because he and the crew hadn't seen the sun or the moon for fourteen days and nights. No one ate, no one slept, and "all hope that we should be saved was now gone," the narrative declares. Then Paul stood up and said that he had been praying and God had assured him that not a man would be lost. While the storm was still raging, he declared, "I believe God, that it shall be even as it was told me" (Acts 27:25). Feelings indicated all were lost. Faith assured all were saved. I give a faith that overcomes feelings. Are you living by faith or feelings? Are you walking in the flesh or by the Spirit?

MEEKNESS. Roman soldiers lashed the flesh of the Savior's back into bloody shreds. They slapped His face and savagely ridiculed Him. Then they cruelly nailed the sinless one to a criminal's cross. "Yet he opened not his mouth" in bitterness or complaint at the unfairness of it all. That's real meekness. Have you been mistreated a little for following Christ? Any complaining on your part? Why don't you ask me for the meekness I alone can give you?

SELF-CONTROL. Ever lose your Christian cool? Think of Paul and Silas! Acts 16 tells the story of their being falsely accused, beaten, thrown into prison, and having their feet locked in the stocks. A perfect time to lose one's Christian cool. In response to their unjust suffering, they did not express anger. They didn't even have mean things to say about those who treated them so cruelly. The Bible says, "They prayed and sang praises unto God." What self control! But it wasn't theirs, it was mine. The self-control I gave them I want to give you. Do you desire to stop losing your cool? Do you want my fruit in place of your failure? Then, let me tell you how to obtain it.

You get it like you got Christ's salvation. You simply took salvation by faith. In the same way you choose to "walk in the Spirit" (Gal. 5:16). The apostle Paul said, "If we live in the Spirit, let us also walk in the Spirit" (Gal. 5:25). As an act of faith, turn yourself (your spirit) over to me so that I can control your life each day. In that way you will walk under my direction. Your conduct will be under my control and my fruit will be seen in your life.

Your friends peg you by the fruit they see in your life. Grapes don't grow on thorn bushes and figs don't grow on thistles. You claim to be a Christian. If the world doesn't see my fruit in your life, it will spot you as a phony. Trust me every day. I alone can make your Christian life and daily conduct real and fruitful—even beautiful.